THE FLIGHT OF A MONARCH

Allison Choi

BookLeaf Publishing

India | USA | UK

The Flight Of A Monarch © 2021 Allison Choi

Presentation by BookLeaf Publishing

Web: www.bookleafpub.com

E-mail: info@bookleafpub.com

ISBN: 9789358738759

First edition 2021

DEDICATION

For you, Emi, and all the dreamers out there. I hope I did you justice.

PREFACE

This is not my story

But of someone

Who I wanted

To give my voice to,

But more than that

It is of anyone

Full of hope

That this land will

Set them free

And to the ones wondering

If they really belong here,

I want you to know

That you do

No matter what they say.

I hope that you will

Read this story

And understand

That even in the land

Of the free

Freedom

Is not always free

And that freedom

Does not ensure

Equality

Even though the definition

Of freedom

Would seem to say otherwise

This country

Has so many flaws,

Yet people flock to it

For a better life

Because it is full of

Promise

And hope,

There is beauty

In all the ugly parts

When you have hope.

We as a country

Are not great despite

Being full of people

Not born on this soil,

We are great because

We are a land of immigrants.

Remember your roots

As Americans were all once

Travelers

Refugees

Wanderers

From a foreign land

Looking for a better life.

If we belong here

Why can't they?

Illegal

they call us illegal,

Illegal

the word haunts me

lives in

the crevices of my brain,

Illegal

I hear them spit angrily

like snakes spitting venom

at their helpless prey,

Illegal

they call me

as if I am a crime

for existing,

Illegal

as if I am better off

dead

than in a country

I was not born in;

does it matter

that I have lived my whole life

on this soil?

That this land is the only one

I can remember?

Illegal

they whisper with flaming eyes

and cry "go back

to where you came from!"

Illegal

but if not here,

where is it that I belong?

Why is it

that they treat me

like I tried to steal their nation

from them,

I was a child brought here

unknowingly,

shall I be punished

for a crime I didn't know

existed?

Should I be punished

for risking my life

to swim across that river?

Illegal

I may be a criminal

in your eyes

but I am not your enemy

unless you force me to be.

Illegal

the word pummels my skull;

they say I am illegal

they wish to strip me

of the things that make me human

by labelling my entire being

as a crime,

but you cannot pretend

that labelling me illegal

strips me of my humanity,

you cannot pretend

that I have come

to disrupt your life;

I am a survivor

a refugee

searching for a way to live

instead of survive

and you shun me

for a crime

I didn't know I was committing?

Illegal

the label haunts me

shadows me

it's burned it in my heart

and I carry it with me

everywhere I go

I just cannot wait

'til the day I get rid of it.

I was too young to remember

how plans were made

what plans were made

if there were plans made,

I was too young to understand

where my mom

had gone.

America

was just a collection

of letters in my brain

but for my mom

it was a way out.

Out of an abusive relationship

from a man

who knocked her up

at seventeen,

out of the country

that had the potential

to mold her beloved son

into his father.

Out

she got out

she sought life

instead of survival

safety

instead of pain

she got out

but left me behind,

left me as long as she

could bear

until I forgot her,

I forgot my own mom.

She did not deserve it

when I mistook

my grandma for my life giver,

it was not her fault

that leaving me behind

was the only way to ensure

her safety

I was too young

to know the pain

of a son forgetting his mom,

too young

to know how strong

my mom was

for surviving,

too young

to understand that

my mom

was not strong enough

to let her baby boy

forget her so soon,

much too young

to know what was happening

to know where I was going

to know that the word

America

would change my life forever,

I was too young to know

who my mom was

I was too young to be making

such a perilous journey,

but I went

unknowingly

following my grandma

to my new future,

America awaited me

We made it

my grandma

pulling me along

swimming

for our lives

for our new lives

for our future lives,

I can still feel

the weight of the water

dragging me

the dark

chilly

currents

flowing around me,

but I do not remember it.

I do not remember,

I only know the feeling

of being reborn

when we surfaced on

the other side;

I take a swimming test

years later

and feel myself floundering

in the big river

instead of the tiny pool,

but I only have these

subconscious feelings

to remind me of my journey

We made it,

but not without strife

We made it,

but I was still found out.

a court summons

appears in the mail

with my misspelled name

plastered on the front,

a court summons

to send me back

for entering illegally.

I am a child and have

no concept of courts

or the law,

it was not my fault

after all

that I got to America,

do you really think

that my little child brain

would think to swim the river

and face the

large

scary

guards

on the other side?

Why is it me

who must go to court

for the actions

I unknowingly committed?

I cannot read the letter

as I barely have a concept

for what English is,

what could I do

besides ignore it?

A young boy

(just a toddling toddler really)

is terrified

of this new land,

it mystifies him

with its ghosts

on the road

every 10 feet,

he sees the

glowing ghost orbs

wiz by,

he shudders as they

flick past ominously

even though he is shielded

by the safety of the car.

He has never seen

a brighter night

than the one filled

with ghosts,

for the nights

were dark

in the small village

he was coming from

and he is already

on edge

from the weary journey;

a journey through

the chill water

that tried to creep into

his lungs,

the journey past

the menacing guards

with gleaming guns

in the distance

(but still too close for comfort),

and the last part

in the loud monster

roaring through the night

plowing by the ghosts

carrying him to his mom

carrying him through hope

that the opportunities

outweigh

the hardships.

It was too much to process

emotions everywhere

left the boy

frazzled enough

to see ghosts

in the streetlamps

(though in his defence,

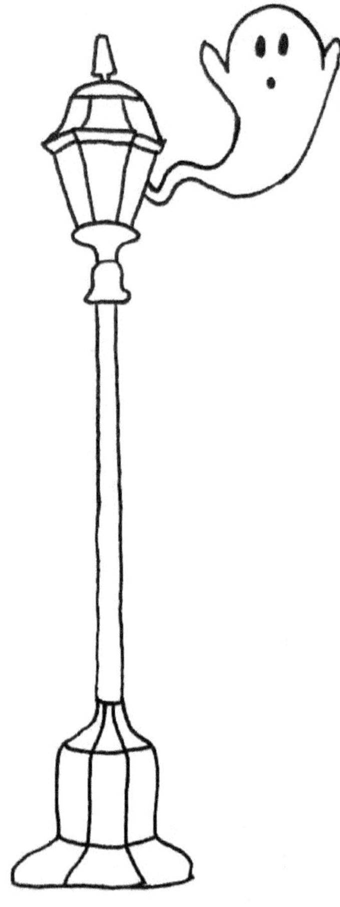

he had never seen

a streetlamp before).

I am him

the boy is me,

yet I never let

the ghosts get me

My mother

my beautiful Hispanic

mamá

got married

despite her past

of abusive men,

despite only just

getting out of her teens

she married

an American

a white man

and he became Dad

I still don't know

whether she married

out of love

or for security,

and I don't know

that I really want

to find out.

My new dad

was the only one

I could remember

calling Dad

and he was there

He was not perfect

(nobody is)

but he was there.

He was there to take me

to boy scouts

where I learned to love

the precious earth

this land

that I called home;

even if its people

rejected me,

nature would always

welcome me home.

He was there

to take me to his work

the large construction sites

filled with mud and trucks

but more importantly

filled with half-finished dreams

and massive skeletons

looming over me,

I was entranced

with the images

of these giants

in the sky

and I wanted so badly

to be part of their

creation;

I wanted to do something

that grand

that impactful

so that many would see

what I was capable of,

He was there

for the formation of my

dreams

my aspirations,

He was there

supporting my family

and some of his own

despite knowing

the threat we imposed.

He was there

simply until

He wasn't.

No my dad was not perfect,

I still flinch

when someone raises

a hand

near me

even if I trust them

not to hit me,

I get chills

when I hear the sound

of a belt being unbuckled

and feel the places where

bright red

welts

stood out on my back,

I still remember

how to make those sandwiches

he would demand from me

around lunchtime

as if I was nothing more than

a servant to his whims,

no

my dad was not perfect

nowhere close

but he was still my dad

the one and only one

who earned that title

until

he

left

me

behind.

No warning,

he was gone

vanished

as a magician in an act,

there was a hole

in our family

and a hole

in my life.

I was fatherless

for the second time

The bastard left

my mom

to support her

and her three sons

herself

when he knew

that her lack of education

and immigrant status

were working so hard

against her,

he knew how

poor

he was leaving us

and yet he left,

left us

left his family

his wife

and his sons

for another woman

and another family,

Were we not enough?

Would we ever be enough?

Would I ever be enough?

I am numb inside

I feel nothing

otherwise I would

shatter into a million pieces,

I feel nothing

because we have to survive

I am the oldest

I am the most responsible

so I absolutely

can't

let myself

feel

anything

as I aimlessly

plod

through life

trying to find

a way up

but my life

has no

purpose

and I

am lost.

I drift away

from my schoolwork

from my peers

I feel stranded

without a lifeline

bobbing in the middle

of a vast sea

it feels like

one of my legs has collapsed

and they drugged me

for the pain

I am empty

devoid of emotion

I have to be

for my family's sake

but my inner turmoil

keeps me awake

Was I not a good enough son?

Is he embarrassed

to be with my family?

Why doesn't he

want me?

My country doesn't want me,

my stepdad doesn't want me,

where do I belong

if not here?

How do I go on

if I am not wanted

anywhere?

He is gone

but I am here

and someday

someday

I'll show the world

that I deserve to be

here

too.

But it feels

so far,

so

far

away

Paralyzed

caught

between sorrow

anger

hatred

I wonder how

the human body is

capable

of so many emotions,

they are not

sustainable.

I am falling apart

even on the

good days

the emotions just

fade

to background noise

simmering

in my mind

waiting for me

to let them

take over;

I want

to turn off my emotions

I want

to be strong

I want

to stop being controlled

by the actions

of others

I want to be

less vulnerable

to the people

I thought I could

trust

I consider

switching off

my emotions

forever

but forever is permanent

I descend rapidly

into the deep

valley

where I can barely

see the sun

I feel so hopeless

trapped

in my own

country

and now

trapped

in my own

mind

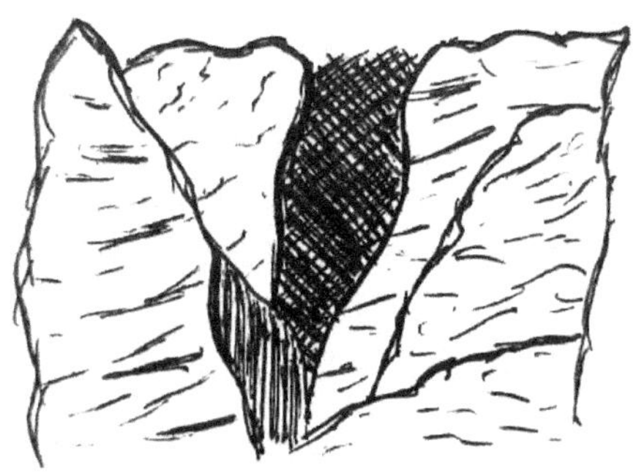

While I was down

in my valley

of misery

I could barely see,

it was so dark

there was

no color.

but when I was there

I saw

my brothers descending

into the darkness

ignoring the opportunity

they were given

and the life

with which

to live it,

and it broke

my heart.

I could not go on

entertaining the darkness

in my mind

while my brothers needed me

to be strong,

I put on a brave face

I felt like I was

a phony

pretender

hiding my true

feelings

but hadn't I lived

my whole life

as a pretender?

It was true

that I was pretending

at first,

but the more

I acted strong

the stronger I

became;

I slowly inched my way

up the walls

of the valley

my mind

had trapped me in,

but the progress

was slow

I would fall

into pitfalls

of anger and hatred

because he

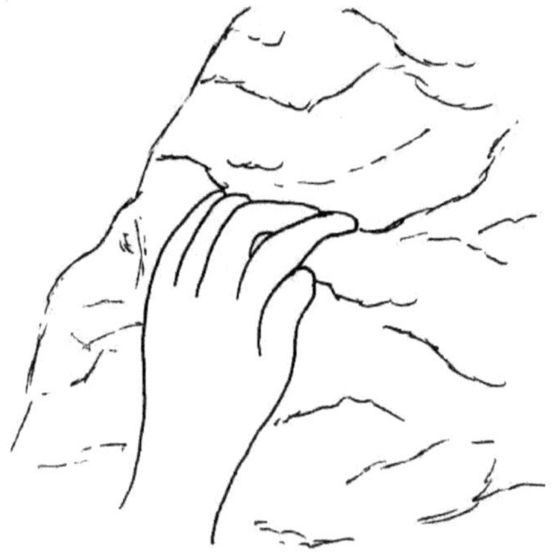

was not

there;

not there

for boy scouts

and certainly not

there

for those

inspiring trips

to the buildings

that were still

halfway

a dream

(I wished they were

my dreams)

he was not there,

not there

for me to rely on

I became an expert

at finding rides

and loyal friends

who would trust me

without ever knowing

my situation,

but I felt

like a beggar

a bum

offering nothing

to get something anyway

every time

I felt like I was stooping

so low

and every time

I felt the anger

well up in me,

he was not there

if only

he was there.

if only

he hadn't

shattered

my trust

like glass,

if only

this was a nightmare

and I could just

wake up.

If only

He was there.

We are poor

abandoned

I am the oldest

I must stay strong

and learn

to provide,

but nobody wants me

a non-American

a foreigner

an immigrant

an illegal?

I search for a way,

but the best I can do

is cut grass

it's nowhere near

enough,

but at least

it's something.

I am barely

out of childhood,

but I know

the responsibility

of adults

the responsibility

for life

responsibility for

things

you have no control over

and the expectations

of those that

look up to you

for you to control

the uncontrollable

I skipped growing up

and became grown,

I left my childhood behind

to survive,

I am an

imposter

trying so hard

to belong

I don't

have the heart

to smile,

I am worn out.

how was I supposed

to know

that it gets better

as I was drowning

in my life?

I feel cheated

tossed around

as if life thinks

it's fun

to play with me

as if I am

a rag doll.

I am lost

searching for better

amongst

the shreds of hope

that I have left

holding on

until a better day

that I don't even know

will come

I do not try

to be distant

I truly wish

I could belong,

but I just can't let

myself

get close to anyone.

I have too much to hide

too many secrets to keep,

I am afraid

that someone will

connect the dots

about my history

if I tell them too much,

I'm afraid

that I will be rejected

cast out

by the home

the people

I want to belong to

that I feel

I belong to

Will they shun me?

Cast me out?

Make me leave?

I fear to even consider

letting anyone get close

enough

to let my questions be answered.

I am missing something

missing out

on childhood friends

and screaming popular songs

with my friends in my car

as we drive to get food

and sleepovers

with kids my mom

would trust,

instead I avoid

hanging out

outside of school

because my mom

told me I couldn't.

I wish I knew

what normal

feels like

what it would be like

to have a normal childhood,

but childhood

is not something

you can redo

and I cannot help

that I was robbed

of normalcy

Sometimes

I wish I knew

what my friends

teachers

classmates

think about me

would they see the

kind heart

that drove me

to take care of my mom

and brothers

during our hardest times?

Would they see the eyes

full of ambition

to learn

and to rise

to become something more

than the world deemed me

to be?

Would they see the work

that I put in to study

for the SATs

all those extra hours

to make up for

my school not

teaching me enough?

Would they see my potential

in every fiber

radiating

out of every pore

searching for a

better life?

Or would they see

a poor kid

that became chubby

because I couldn't

afford

anything but cheap

unhealthy

food?

A poor kid who wore

the same few

bulky sweatshirts

on loop

because buying new clothes

was too frivolous

for me?

Or how about the kid

hiding his hands

in his sleeves

covering them with the

loose fabric

so no one could see

my extra finger

that I was too poor

to get removed?

(nevermind that I

couldn't even see

an American doctor

and had no insurance)

Was it possible

for them to see both?

The battle between

my ambition

my potential

my limited education

and my lack of money

holding me back?

It's sad to say

that there were probably

people who saw me

as nothing more

than the poor kid

(and they were not wrong)

but I had more determination

than all of them combined

to make use of this country's

ability to rise.

My mom wanted a better

life

for me

and though it may not

have seemed

as if this was any better,

I just had to get out

of this town

I had to

get out

of this suffocating

situation,

I had to get out

I had to

I love my mom

so much more

than most things

of this world,

she took the risk

to get herself here

then took the risk

to get me here

even if that meant

waiting for me to follow.

I don't remember

my town

or my old life

in another country,

but my mom does

and she thought it was

limiting enough

to get out.

My mom

always wanted

a better education

than the one she got,

the schools

she could go to

were too far away that

she could not go

and it crushed her soul,

she would not let the same

happen to her sons.

I cannot say

that my education

was very great,

it was difficult

because I could not just

go home

and ask my parents

for homework help

I had to learn

to speak up for myself

and find ways

to get the help I needed,

yet

my mom

never stopped

encouraging me

from pursuing education,

and I

never stopped

encouraging her

to go back to school

to get her GED

(which she is doing)

and to study for the

citizenship test

(which she passed!)

because we both understood

the power

of education

she wanted me to look

at college,

something that was not

possible

for her

even though we only

had pennies

to our names

I had to find out

about the whole

application process myself:

how to write entry essays

where to apply

when to apply

which schools to look at

what to consider as my major

how to get scholarships

how to apply

for financial aid

as a non-citizen.

Hours

and hours

of research

by myself,

there were so many things

dividing

me,

a first-gen,

from kids who

were primed to go

to college

from the day

they were born

but I was not guaranteed

acceptance into college,

my destiny

was held by

the people deciding

if an immigrant

was worth

giving a chance

The hours

of research

would be all

for naught

if I couldn't even

get in,

so I waited

patiently

anxiously

this was my shot

to get out

this was my chance

to show that I could

do it,

this was my chance

to follow my dreams

to do something

grand

with my life

if only I could get in.

However

acceptance

is only one step

of the way forward

as I cannot pay,

I cannot afford it

even if I am accepted

I'm hoping

for a miracle

for some empathy

some compassion

to carry me through,

I wait

trying not to think

of the worst

praying

for just one thing

to go right.

My fate hangs

on tenuous strings

and on the

fraying vine

I grabbed

desperately

to swing me across

the river that separates

me from

my dreams.

I just hope

that I did enough

that I gave enough

of myself

away

for them

to want me

for them to lend me

a sturdier vine

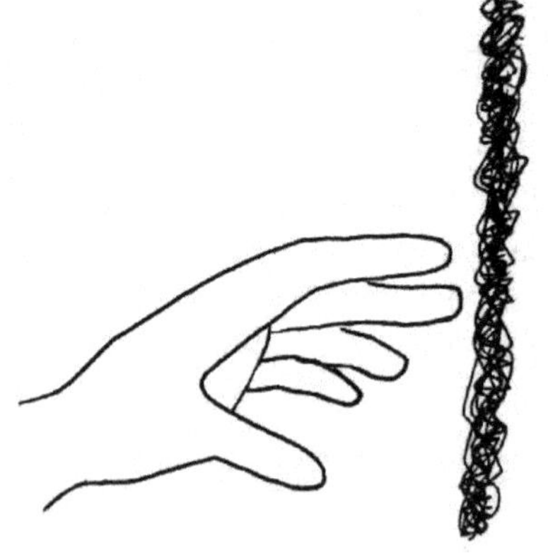

to get me across

I'm hoping

that I don't drown

or remain stuck

on this side,

this is my shot

I just hope

it was worth it

I just hope

I am enough,

all of my life

I have wanted

to be

enough

and this is

the moment

of truth

I am lonely

for I cannot truly

be myself

without exposing

all my secrets

lonely

because I am not allowed

to hang out

after school

lonely

because I am trying

to do something

that no one in my family

has done before

lonely

because I don't know

who to talk to

about college

lonely

because I have to spend

all this time

finding the answers

for myself

lonely

because I know

I can only trust myself

lonely

because no one understands

when I talk about school

at home

lonely

because my family

as much as they

support

and care

have no concept

of college

lonely

because I am the first

in my family

but so far behind

my classmates

in everything besides

schoolwork

lonely

because I don't look

like the people

I'm surrounded by

lonely

I have no one

to wait with

who is as anxious as me

to get into college

lonely

because I set my sights

higher than

state school

lonely

I feel like

I am the only one

who knows

they are trapped

and have to get out

lonely

because I need to rise

even if that means

I leave it all behind

lonely

because I have to be

alone

to survive

lonely

after my dad

broke my trust

I have never relied

on anyone besides

myself

I walk

a lonely road

I wish I could share it

I wish there was someone

for me to share it with

I want to be

understood

I want to be

I watched

as the rejections rolled in

with their

"we regret to inform you"

and

"we were impressed

with your application,

however,"

and I felt like

my vine was unraveling fast

and I was almost ready

to let the river

claim me for its own,

I was grasping at vines

only to find out

that they were nothing more

than hallucinations

my mind created

did I really

overestimate myself

that much?

I wanted to be strong

but I was walking

in shadow

I let myself succumb

to the dark clouds

that had been hovering

around

for all those years,

I absorbed the dark clouds

held them inside of me

and let them

fill me entirely.

I remember

one night

we were out too late,

me and my stepbrother

enjoying the cool air

as the day became night

letting the wind

blow through our hair

across our skin

as we biked down the

slope of our street.

We were not supposed

to be out

it was almost night

and night

was not forgiving

where I lived,

I should've known

better

but the next thing I knew

I was facedown

in a ditch

my bike lying

feet away from me

and I could not move

and I could not feel

anything besides

blinding pain

the night was dark

but the pain was blinding

the night was dark

so I had to get home

I gritted my teeth

picked myself

and my beaten bike

up out of the ditch

and rode home

with only one hand

the only one

capable

of holding

the handlebar.

I had fractured my wrist

maybe broken it,

I had no insurance

I had no identity

with the government

I could not go

to the hospital

I could not get anything

to ease the pain

besides my mother

whispering to me

"the greater the difficulty,

the greater the glory"

but even this

did not help me

from wondering

where the glory was

in a broken wrist

and feeling the pain

of my mistakes.

But now

I came home

to another letter

from another college

I had lost almost

all of my hope

but I could not lose it

entirely

or I would have

no reason

to keep going.

I did not expect much

after my previous

failures

but I opened it

to find

the words

that would change everything,

"Welcome to the class

of 2022!"

I read the words

and almost wept

with relief

and joy

I had made it

I was enough

I was wanted

I was here

I was alive

I could become something

or someone,

it felt as if

I was pulling myself

out of that ditch

all over again

but this time

I was blinded

by hope

instead of pain

and this time

my mom wrapped me in

her most exuberant

hug

instead of wrapping

my injured wrist

I could see it now mom!

I could see the glory!

I was blinded,

blinded

by the glory!

I had gotten in

I really did

me

I did

it was not fake

it was very real

I did it

they wanted me!

it was a big hurdle

but it was not

the only hurdle

blocking my path

for I still

couldn't

pay.

I submitted

whatever financial documents

I could

and explained my situation;

if I thought I felt

like a beggar before

it was nothing

compared to this

and luckily

they understood everything

even though

I did not have DACA

(my parents

didn't know to sign me up)

or really anything

besides my ability

to appeal to their compassion

but they listened

and I'll never forget

that they helped me

escape

from my old life

for the second time

for so long

I questioned

how this was the land

of the free

how this was the land

where people could

be free

when I was nowhere

close

to freedom

and I had lived here

almost all my life.

I was still

so limited

with what I could do

in this country,

I was not free

even after coming

to the land of the free,

I did not understand

how this was a land

of opportunity

when I was denied

an existence here,

but I existed anyway

I thrived

flourished

on the soil

where freedom

was fought for,

without ever really

knowing the freedom

of being American,

it was only when

I knew I was going

to college

that I finally understood

that this was a land

of opportunity

a land

of freedom

even if

I was not

free yet

it was progress

it was hope

it was a way

to build a new life

a better life

it was more

than hope

it was a guaranteed

future

I laid in bed

staring at the ceiling

hoping to fall asleep

but the jittering

of my nerves

made it difficult

to relax.

Tomorrow was the day

that I would begin again

and I was nervous

I didn't know

if I had what I needed

I didn't know

if anyone would want

to be friends with me

I didn't know

how hard the classes would be

I had no one

to tell me

what to expect

but I couldn't show

what I was feeling

I had to act like

I knew what I was doing

or else

I would fall apart

I left in the summer

for a program

to help me

get a head start

on the transition from

high school

to college

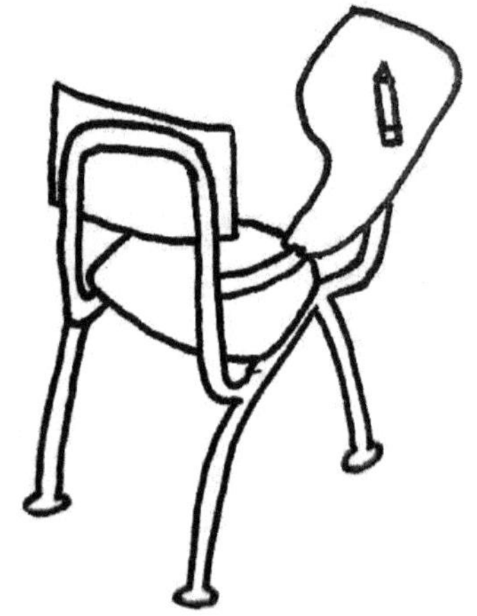

and it was like

I was slapped

in the face.

I felt so very

alive

and finally felt

like I belonged

but I still

was so far behind,

it was overwhelming

in the most

exciting way

I met so many people

who were like me,

who also struggled

with stability

and security

and even

for the first time

I found people

who understood

what it was like

to have to sneak around

the government,

to have to deal with

being called illegal

and being made less

of a human

because we were not

born here.

I finally knew

I was not alone

I finally had people

to share everything with,

but I had trouble still

letting myself trust them

I didn't know

how to study with them

I didn't even know

how to study on my own

I didn't know

how to talk about

my issues

and let myself

open up

I had a place in this world

and it was here,

but somehow

I was still struggling

with the weight

of my past

and how little prepared

my high school left me

to deal with the

intensity

of college,

I was here

and struggling still

but at least now

I could see

that my struggle

would amount to something

there were people

here

that understood

all that I had to bear.

I would make it

I would learn

I would do my best

and make my family

proud

I had a place

I belonged

I had people

who were like me

I still felt

out of place.

I was one of the only

Hispanic students

in my high school

I was surrounded

by white

conservative

southerners,

(not that there is

anything

wrong with that)

but I missed out

on my culture,

I was taken

from my "homeland"

and this new land

became my home

but I still

longed

for a place to

identify with,

I certainly did not

fit in

in my school,

unfortunately,

they were the only

culture

I remember.

I went to college

and was surrounded

by people who

shared my

ethnicity,

yet I did not

have the same culture

as them

I did not quite

fit in

and it made me regret

my upbringing.

I turned a blind eye

to everything I used to be

grateful for

instead I picked out the faults

and wished they were different

but the thing about the past

is that it can't be changed

only forgotten

or accepted

And then I met her

Not to be cliché,

but I never thought

one person

had the ability

to change my

whole life

until I met her.

Until I borrowed her pencil

and proceeded to lose it,

(accidentally of course)

she somehow

forgave me and

became my Amie

and I was her Emi.

In so many ways

she was like me

sure she was not

Hispanic

or even

undocumented,

but she knew

what it felt like

to have a lost identity

she was also

searching

for some kind

of culture

she had lost amidst

her small town home.

This was it

I spent so long

feeling as if

I was not enough

as if I was

too different

as if I was

a puzzle piece

trying to fit

in the wrong puzzle

but so was she

and so were we

I never found

the puzzle I belonged to

but I fit with her

Emi and Amie,

and that was enough

that will be enough.

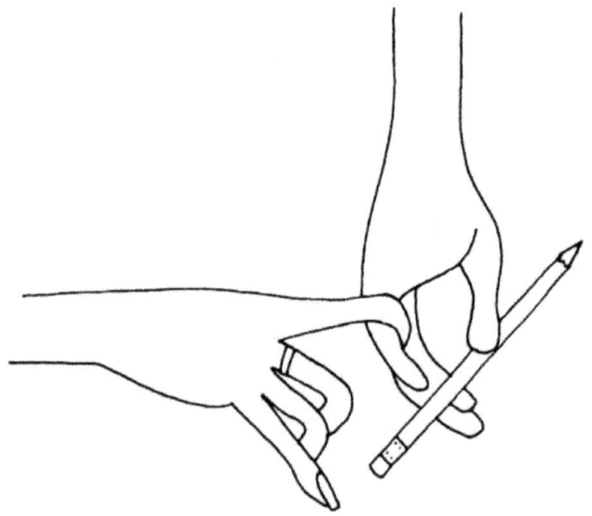

I never asked

for life

none of us ever

wanted it

until we suddenly

got it

and now what?

We live

but what does it mean

to live?

I had to fight

for my right

to live a good life

while there are so many

who did not have

the same opportunity

as me.

How are there

so many degrees

of life?

I made it

the hard way

I had to learn what

pain was

in order to

love living,

I have lived my whole life

in a limbo

and even if

I can get DACA

or apply for a green card

through my mom,

I will still be stuck

as an immigrant in this country

for many more years,

a subscriber to a place

that will take its time

to accept me.

But it is not

all hopeless,

here I am

accepted to

grad school

and I have saved enough

to be able to go,

I am so lucky

just to be here

just to be alive

I am almost done

with undergrad

Where did the time go?

I am glad to have been here

and learned so much

it is bittersweet

that I cannot live

in these moments

forever

except what is preserved

in my memory

pressed in

the loose associations

of my brain

time goes forward

and so do I

what can I do

besides live

in the now

and appreciate

how far I

was able to come?

And how far

I may now

be able to go?

I am contained

in the flight of

the Monarchs

the long

perilous

journey

taken to survive,

I am the Monarchs

on their flight

changing

fighting

to make it

to a better place,

it is not one journey

it is a cycle.

Even if I

do not return home

I can never forget

where I came from

for it is a part of me,

the cycle continues

as I migrate to learn

and am humbled by

my upbringing,

the duality

of being both foreign

and American

is the cycle

of the Monarchs

and this is just

one flight

in a lifetime

of migrations

ACKNOWLEDGEMENTS

I have always hoped in some small part of me that I could be capable of writing a book and weaving a story as well as my favorite authors could, though I never imagined that I would one day write a book of poems! And though I told very few that I was working on this work, there are so many people that deserve to be acknowledged for supporting and encouraging me through everything I do.

I want to first thank my wonderful family: Mom, Dad, Anna, and Becca for always believing in me and encouraging me to do what my heart desires. I am so thankful to have you and would not have made it this far without your love and support. Special thanks to Becca for putting up with my last-minute requests to look over these poems and to Anna for helping me illustrate the poems and for designing a wonderful cover. Also, to my friend Kirsten Malsam for having in-depth conversations with me about books and exposing me to a world of literature that inspired me to write and tell stories of my own. To her and Hallie Malsam, I want to thank for loving and supporting me like they were my own family.

As a college student writing these poems during the semester, I want to also thank Leah Truskinovsky and Janice Ko for making my workload feel a little lighter. I would not be able to survive in college without them or the way they brighten my life.

And finally, for Emi for letting me give a voice to your story. I really could not have done this without all those late-night questions about your life, those deep discussions about your feelings during each major event in your life, and all the time you spent looking over the poems and making sure they captured your story well. Thank you for encouraging me to live out my dreams and help make them a tangible reality.